Dropping In On...
INDONESIA

Christina J. Moose

A Geography Series

THE ROURKE BOOK COMPANY, INC.
VERO BEACH, FLORIDA 32964

Printed in the United States of America

**Library of Congress
Cataloging-in-Publication Data**

Moose, Christina J., 1952-
    Indonesia / Christina J. Moose.
        p. cm. — (Dropping in on)
    Includes bibliographical references and index.
    Summary: Briefly describes some of the major cities and regions of Indonesia, as well as its people, foods, animal life, and more.
    ISBN 1-55916-281-3
    1. Indonesia—Juvenile literature. [1. Indonesia—
    Description and travel.] I. Series.

DS615 .M68 2000
959.8—dc21

                                    00-025282

Printed in the USA

Indonesia
■ ■ ■ ■ ■ ■ ■ ■ ■ ■ ■

Official Name: Republic of Indonesia

Area: 741,096 square miles
(1,919,439 square kilometers)

Population: 216 million

Capital: Jakarta

Largest City: Jakarta
(population 8.5 million)

Highest Elevation: Puncak Jaya,
16,503 feet (5,030 meters)

Official Language: Bahasa Indonesia

Major Religion: Islam

Money: Rupiah

Form of Government: Multiparty republic

Flag:

TABLE OF CONTENTS

Our Blue Ball — The Earth

The Earth can be divided into two hemispheres. The word hemisphere means "half a ball"—in this case, the ball is the Earth.

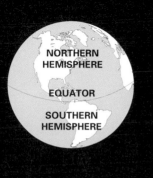

The equator is an imaginary line that runs around the middle of the Earth. It separates the Northern Hemisphere from the Southern Hemisphere. North America— where Canada, the United States, and Mexico are located—is in the Northern Hemisphere.

The Equatorial Zone

When the North Pole is tilted toward the sun, the sun's most powerful rays strike the northern half of the Earth and the people in the Northern Hemisphere enjoy summer. When the North Pole is tilted away from the sun, winter comes to the Northern Hemisphere, and it is summer in the Southern Hemisphere.

At the equator, the sun shines the same for most of the year. In countries near the equator, winter and summer are both warm. Seasons may have different amounts of rain, but they are usually alike in temperature.

Get Ready for Indonesia

Let's take a trip! Climb into your hot-air balloon, and we'll drop in on a country that stretches along one-eighth of Earth's equator. Indonesia is the largest nation in Southeast Asia and the biggest *archipelago* in the world: a group of 13,000 islands stretching 3,200 miles (5,100 kilometers) from the Indian to the Pacific Ocean.

Millions of years ago, three pieces of Earth's surface crunched together to make the mountains, volcanoes, jungles, and seas that form Indonesia.

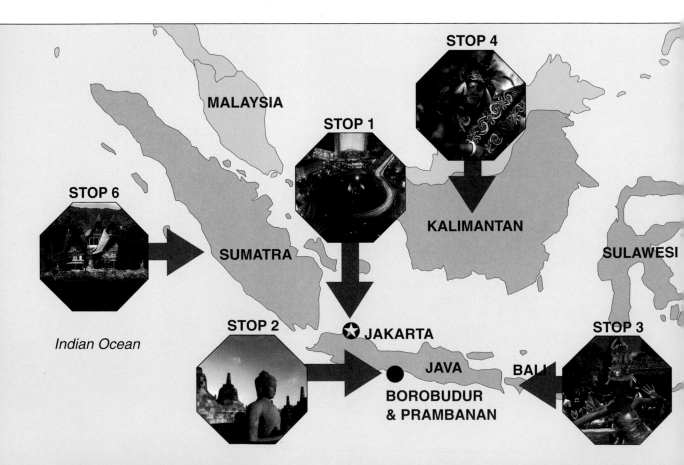

MALAYSIA

STOP 4

STOP 1

STOP 6

KALIMANTAN

SUMATRA

SULAWESI

Indian Ocean

STOP 2

JAKARTA

STOP 3

JAVA

BALI

BOROBUDUR
& PRAMBANAN

The plants and animals from Asia and Australia also came together: rhinoceroses, orangutans, giant insects, the *Rafflesia* (the biggest and smelliest flower in the world), and even a dragon!

Today, Indonesia is a land of great beauty, modern cities, and ancient cultures, but also problems: No one is quite sure what will happen as this huge, multicultural nation enters the twenty-first century.

STOP 5

Pacific Ocean

N
W E
S

IRIAN JAYA

Indonesia

★ National Capital

500 miles

804.65 km

Stop 1: Jakarta

Jakarta, the capital, is on the northwest coast of Java, where half of all Indonesians live. Each year, thousands of people from the countryside come to Jakarta seeking jobs, and sometimes they go home to visit their families. The city's population is therefore hard to count, but it may be as much as 14 million.

Like the rest of Indonesia, Jakarta is a mixture of old and new. It is a modern city with both skyscrapers and slums. Fancy cars and hotels line its wide boulevards, but foot-carts and tin shacks crowd its unpaved streets. The city is hot, humid, and crowded. In the monsoon season, when it rains for days or weeks, parts of the city are flooded.

Batavia was the capital when the Dutch ruled Indonesia in the 1800's. Today tourists visit Batavia to see the old Dutch buildings, the fish market, and the *wayang* (puppet) museum.

*Now let's fly **southeast** to Borobudur and Prambanan.*

Jakarta by night with its "Welcome Statue" at the center of a modern traffic roundabout.

Unity in Diversity?

Indonesia's motto is "Unity in Diversity." *Diversity* means "having many different things." In this case, the different things are different people.

It's easy to see why Indonesia is so diverse: Its population, the fifth largest in the world, includes 300 ethnic groups speaking 365 languages. They descend from Malay peoples, Pacific islanders, and tribal groups. These people mixed with foreigners from China, Arabia, India, and Europe—especially the Portuguese and Dutch.

Its great size and diversity make Indonesia a culturally rich country, but diversity has caused problems, too. Indonesia is still trying to build enough roads, telephones, and businesses to provide for all its people. Also, many of its people have different religions and traditions.

Some people want to break away from Indonesia and build their own countries. In 1999, there was so much fighting between the East Timorese people and Indonesian soldiers that the United Nations sent a group of Australians to stop the violence.

Indonesia is a diverse nation of many different peoples.

A statue of a praying Buddha rises at the middle of Borobudur Temple, surrounded by domed stupas.

Stop 2: Borobudur and Prambanan

In the middle of Java, two ancient Hindu-Buddhist temples stand near the city of Yogyajakarta. Borobudur took 10,000 men 100 years to build. It was finished more than 1,100 years ago. It is a *stupa*, a domed shrine to the Hindu god Buddha. Pictures called *reliefs* are carved into its stone walls. They show the life of Buddha, and 432 statues of Buddha sit above these reliefs. At the very top are carvings that show Buddha's rise to heaven.

Prambanan is a group of temples and buildings built at about the same time. There were once 244 temples, but only 16 have been saved from the forest that grew over them. Together, these temples are dedicated to the Hindu god Shiva, but each temple is devoted to a different *deity* (god). Carvings in temple walls tell the tales of the *Ramayana*, a famous story from India.

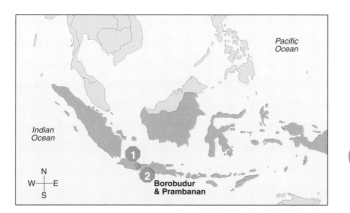

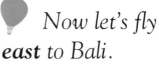 *Now let's fly east to Bali.*

Stop 3: Bali

Bali is one of the prettiest islands in the world. Volcanoes rise high at its center, surrounded by terraces of rice paddies, flower-filled rain forests, and waterfalls. The Balinese are famous for their kindness, beauty, and spirituality.

The Balinese people believe that everything, even a flower, has a spirit. They make offerings to the gods to ward off evil, and they wear sashes to keep evil from rising up to their heads. Stone figures called *garudas* protect their houses and temples.

Bali is the home of the famous Balinese dancers. Women dressed in gold with flowered headdresses perform dances that retell stories from the *Ramayana* and *Mahabharata*, two ancient books from India. They kneel, making slow, circular movements with their hands and eyes. Men dance with stronger movements. As they dance, a *gamelan* orchestra plays gongs, bamboo flutes, and two-stringed instruments.

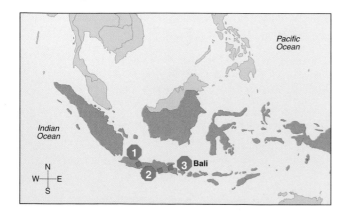

Now let's fly **north** *to Kalimantan.*

This young Balinese girl is performing a special dance called the rejang.

Stop 4: Kalimantan

Kalimantan is Indonesia's part of Borneo, the third largest island in the world. Mangrove trees grow in swamps on the southern coast, with jungles, rivers, and mountains in the center. A beautiful forest of orchids near the village of Melak covers 5,000 acres (2023 hectares). Oil refineries line the coast, and loggers are bulldozing the forests for wood, so the government protects bear cats, monkeys, and orangutans in Tanjung Puting National Park.

Borneo was once famous for its head hunters and *cannibals* (people who eat other people), but these practices were never very common, and today they no longer occur. Instead, the Dayak people, who live near the center, grow crops and put on shows for the tourists.

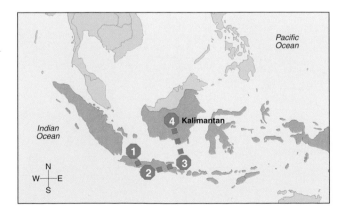

Now let's fly ***southeast*** *to Sulawesi.*

A Dayak musician from the province of Kalimantan, on the island of Borneo.

The Komodo Dragon

The jungles of the Indonesian islands are home to many rare and wonderful animals, including elephants, tigers, monkeys, and giant insects like "walking sticks," "walking leaves," and the luna moth. Some of these, like the rhinoceros and the orangutan of Sumatra, are *endangered species* because their jungle-homes are being destroyed by farmers and loggers.

Of all the animals in Indonesia, none is stranger than the Komodo dragon. This lizard lives on only two islands, Komodo and Rinca. Scientists believe that the Komodo dragon is a prehistoric creature from the dinosaur days. Komodo dragons can grow to be 12 feet long and weigh nearly 300 pounds (136 kilograms). When they are hungry, they can be very fierce, so they do not make good pets!

Above: The fierce Komodo dragon can grow to 12 feet and is very fierce when hungry.

Right: Orangutans are very smart. They are found on Sumatra and other Indonesian islands, but they are an endangered species, because farmers and loggers are clearing their jungle-homes.

Stop 5: Sulawesi

Sulawesi—shaped like the letter K and connected at the center by volcanoes—was formed over millions of years as pieces of Antarctica and Australia pushed together. It lies in the eastern half of Indonesia, between the Moluccas (the "spice" islands) and the giant island of Borneo.

The Toraja people live in the mountainous center of Sulawesi and make their living growing rice and breeding pigs. Their houses, called *tongkonans*, stand on stilts above the ground and have curved roofs. The Torajas also carve *tau-taus*, wooden figures that guard graves.

When a Toraja person dies, family and friends arrange a funeral that is really a big party. They invite hundreds of people to dance, sing, feast, and watch bullfights. They kill pigs, chickens, and water buffalos and offer these animals as *sacrifices*. They believe that these animals will go with the dead person's spirit to heaven.

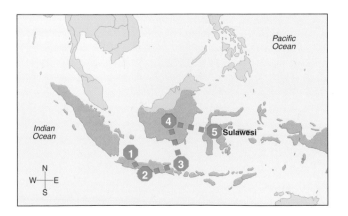

Now let's fly **west** to Sumatra.

A Toraja boy from Sulawesi carries rice bundles. Many Toraja people make a living by growing rice and breeding pigs.

Growing Up in Indonesia

More than half of all Indonesians are under 30 years old. Most children attend elementary school, even if they must travel by boat. Some children also go to high school. Only a few attend college. Even if they do not complete elementary school, 80% of the population can read and write by age 15.

Although Hinduism and Buddhism are strong in Indonesian culture, children are more likely to be part of a Muslim family: Islam, the Muslim religion, is practiced by 88% of Indonesians. Islam is most strictly practiced in the western islands, where families pray every day and sometimes fast, which is going without food for awhile. Most Indonesian Muslims, however, are not so strict.

Many Indonesians live in the countryside. Children in these villages work in the rice fields, herd animals, or fish. As they grow older they may leave the family to seek modern jobs in Jakarta or other big cities.

Most Indonesian children attend some elementary school—even if they
must travel there by boat.

A Batak child with a
water buffalo.

Stop 6: Sumatra

Sumatra is a long, large island the size of California. To the east is the country Malaysia, and in some ways the northern part of Sumatra, Aceh, is like it. In fact, many people in Aceh are fighting to form their own country.

The eastern side of Sumatra is a long plain with oil fields and rubber plantations. The western side has mountains running from north to south. In the north is Lake Toba, the biggest lake in Southeast Asia.

Sumatra is full of active volcanoes. Near its southern tip is the famous volcano Krakatau. In 1883, Krakatau erupted and killed 36,000 people. The smoke and soot filled the Earth's air for more than two years. That eruption created a new volcano, which is still active today!

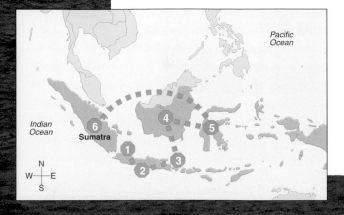

Now it's time to set sail for home.

The Batak people live in these traditional houses in the north of
Sumatra, on Lake Toba.

The Foods of Indonesia

Indonesians like many foods, including noodles (*mie*), chicken (*ayam*), fish (*ikan*), and vegetables. Sometimes Indonesian food is similar to Chinese food, but many Indonesians, like the Padangs of Sumatra, have their own special dishes.

Nasi (rice), the biggest crop, is eaten with every meal, often as *nasi goreng* (fried rice). *Satay*, pieces of meat fried on a long stick and served with peanut sauce, is often eaten with *sambal*, a spicy relish made with chiles. *Gado-gado*—bean sprouts and other vegetables in peanut sauce—goes with many meals. At traditional feasts, *ikan* (fish) is wrapped in banana leaves and grilled or baked.

For dessert, Indonesians eat fruit: papayas, pineapples, custard apples, guavas, mangoes, starfruits, and spiny red rambutans.

Indonesia boasts many delicious tropical fruits, such as these spiny durians.

Indonesia has many special meals that can be found only here, such as these Padang dishes from Sumatra.

Glossary

archipelago   a group of islands

deity   a god

endangered species   a whole group of animals that might die because of human practices

gamelan orchestra   Balinese musicians playing gongs, flutes, and drums

garuda   a stone figure that represents a guardian spirit

relief   a picture carved into stone

stupa   a domed shrine to the god Buddha

tau-tau   a wooden figure that guards a grave

tongkonan   a traditional Toraja house

Further Reading

Berg, Elizabeth. *Indonesia*. Milwaukee: Gareth Stevens, 1997.

Cramer, Mark, and Frederick Fisher. *Indonesia*. Milwaukee: Gareth Stevens, 2000.

Dalton, Bill. *Indonesia*. New York: Odyssey Pubns., 1999.

Lyle, Garry. *Indonesia*. New York: Chelsea House, 1998.

McNair, Sylvia. *Indonesia*. Chicago: Children's Press, 1993.

Martin, James. *Komodo Dragons: Giant Lizards of Indonesia*. Minneapolis: Capstone Press, 1995.

Ryan, Patrick. *Indonesia*. Plymouth, Minn.: Child's World, 1998.

Suggested Web Sites

ArchipelaGo
http://www.goarchi.com/archo/index.html

Indonesian Homepage
http://indonesia.elga.net.id

Let's Go Indonesia
http://lgi.i-2.co.id

Index

Acknowledgments and Photo Credits
All photos: ©Asiafoto. Maps: Moritz Design.